LIVES
AND
TIMES

Diana, Princess of Wales

Haydn Middleton

Heinemann Library
Chicago, Illinois

Designed by Ken Vail Graphic Design, Cambridge
Illustrations by Oxford illustrators
Printed in Hong Kong / China

02 01 00 [or as appropriate]
10 9 8 7 6 5 4 3 2

T 40394

Library of Congress Cataloging-in-Publication Data
Middleton, Haydn.
    Diana, Princess of Wales / Haydn Middleton.
        p.   cm. -- (Lives and times)
    Includes bibliographical references and index.
    ISBN 1-57572-715-3 (lib. bdg.)
    1. Diana, Princess of Wales, 1961– 2. Princesses--Great
Britain--Biography   I. Title. II. Series: Lives and Times
DA591.A45D5345   1998
941.085'092--dc21
    [B]   97-49616
                                                                        CIP

Acknowledgments

The Publishers would like to thank the following for permission to reproduce photographs:

cover photo: Pool, Camera Press

Chris Honeywell pp. 17, 21, 22; Remember When p. 16, reproduced with permission of Mirror Group
Newspapers; Rex Features: p. 19, T. Rooke p. 18, P. Brooker p. 20; Sygma: M. Polak p. 23

Every effort has been made to contact copyright holders of any material reproduced in this book.
Any omissions will be rectified in subsequent printings if notice is given to the Publisher.

All royalties from the sale of this book go to the Diana Memorial Fund.

Some words are shown in bold, **like this**. You can find out what they mean by
looking in the glossary.

Contents

Part One

Diana Spencer was born in 1961, in England. Her family was very wealthy and important. As a young girl, she sometimes played with the children of the Queen of England.

When Diana was sixteen years old, she got
a job in London, England. She helped to look
after young children at a kindergarten.

In 1981, when Diana was nineteen, she married Prince Charles. Charles was Queen Elizabeth's oldest son. He was called the **Prince of Wales**. Diana became the Princess of Wales.

The wedding was in London. People all over
the world watched it on television. Many
people thought Diana looked like a
princess from a fairytale.

Diana and Prince Charles traveled all over the world. Crowds gathered around to meet the young Princess of Wales. People liked her because she was friendly and kind.

In 1982, Diana had a baby son named
William. When Charles dies, William will
become king. Two years later, in 1984,
Diana had a second son, Harry.

As Princess of Wales, Diana wanted to help people who were poor or sick. Most of all, she enjoyed helping children.

Diana visited hospital patients in many different countries. She raised a lot of money that was used to help people in need.

People liked to read about all the things Diana did. Often the newspaper **reporters** and photographers bothered Diana too much. This made her unhappy.

Being the Princess of Wales was very hard work. Also, she was not getting along well with Prince Charles. In 1996, they were **divorced**.

On August 31, 1997, Diana was killed in a car crash in Paris, France. She was only 36 years old. Thousands of people went to put flowers outside her home in London.

More than a million **mourners** went to her **funeral.** She was one of the most popular members of the royal family ever.

Part Two

There are many ways to find out about Diana. From 1981 to 1997, stories about her were printed in the newspapers. Libraries keep copies of old newspapers for people to read.

Many books about Diana were **published** when she was alive. This book was published in 1992. Diana and her friends told the writer all about her life.

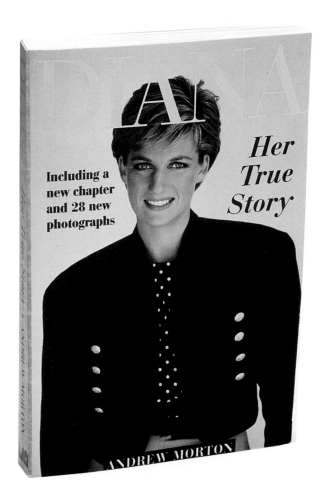

Television **reporters** often filmed Diana on her travels. We can watch these films to find out how Diana looked and talked. Here she is meeting people in Bosnia, in 1997, where there was a war.

Photographers even took photos of Diana when she was on vacation. This made her angry. This photo shows her hiding from photographers with her son Harry.

When Diana died, even people who had never met her felt very sad. They gave **tributes** to show their **respect** for her. This card was fixed to a bunch of flowers.

The pop star, Elton John, played a tribute song to Diana at her **funeral**. It was called "Candle in the Wind." Millions of people bought records of the song, and most of the money went to **charity**.

Many people liked to collect things that have Diana's picture. In 1981, when she was married to Prince Charles, mugs and books like these were sold.

Visitors can now see Diana's childhood home at Althorp, England. Her grave is on this tiny island on the grounds of the Spencer family house.

Glossary

charity to give help or money to people in need

divorced stopped being married

funeral religious ceremony that celebrates the life of someone who has died

mourners people who are sad when someone dies

Prince of Wales oldest son of the king or queen of England who will one day be king.

published printed and put on sale

reporters people who write in newspapers or speak about news on television

respect to value someone because of the things they do

tributes something said, written, or done to show respect for a person

More Books to Read

You can ask an older reader to help you read these books.

Krulik, Nancy. *Princess Diana: Glitter, Glamour, and a Lot of Hard Work.* New York: Scholastic Inc., 1993.

Giff, Patricia. *Diana. Twentieth Century Princess.* New York: Puffin Books, 1992.